"When Paul Willis writes, *'the confused but steady luster of dawn, / clear skies born from gasp of night, / the breathless story,'* he encapsulates the faith and beauty of his new collection. Here, we do not travel through time, as one might suppose, but hold it in abeyance, that prayer might reach each generational corner and poetry fulfill its call. And all the *'inarticulate occasions'* are suddenly blessed by word."

—SOFIA M. STARNES
Virginia Poet Laureate
Poetry Editor for *The Anglican Theological Review*

"A Paul Willis poem is a balm for the tired heart: the breath of a sleeping child, an FDNY hero climbing stairs, a walk through the Glacier Peak Wilderness with the healing 'sound of rivers in our ears.' With both reverence and wit, Willis finds the glint (and sometimes explosion) of joy in all of his travels, from a classroom window to Sawtooth Ridge. *Say This Prayer Into the Past*: your field guide to life and beauty."

—TANIA RUNYAN
Editor, *Every Day Poems*

"Whatever Willis touches on these pages quickens under his wry, wise gaze, and becomes vividly 'green with life.' In both open and fixed forms, he follows his own dictate 'to make sure of the meanings of words, then to invest them with holiness.' His poems are a most welcome and needed gift—a balm he offers to 'this beautiful, suffering world.'"

—PAULANN PETERSEN
Oregon Poet Laureate

"Judging by the poems in 'Antediluvian Baseball,' the final section of his astonishing new collection, one suspects Paul Willis could write brilliantly about *anything*—in heaven, or here on our 'beautiful, suffering world.' Above all, he is a poet with a keen eye and ear for the wonders of Nature's 'understory,' the layer of growth beneath a forest's canopy where 'There is / so much you will never see.' Fear not, reader: Paul Willis will show it to you."

—DAVID STARKEY
Santa Barbara Poet Laureate, Emeritus
Director, Creative Writing Program, Santa Barbara City College

SAY THIS PRAYER INTO THE PAST

The Poiema Poetry Series

Poems are windows into worlds; windows into beauty, goodness, and truth; windows into understandings that won't twist themselves into tidy dogmatic statements; windows into experiences. We can do more than merely peer into such windows; with a little effort we can fling open the casements, and leap over the sills into the heart of these worlds. We are also led into familiar places of hurt, confusion, and disappointment, but we arrive in the poet's company. Poetry is a partnership between poet and reader, seeking together to gain something of value—to get at something important.

Ephesians 2:10 says, "We are God's workmanship . . ." *poiema* in Greek—the thing that has been made, the masterpiece, the poem. The Poiema Poetry Series presents the work of gifted poets who take Christian faith seriously, and demonstrate in whose image we have been made through their creativity and craftsmanship.

These poets are recent participants in the ancient tradition of David, Asaph, Isaiah, and John the Revelator. The thread can be followed through the centuries—through the diverse poetic visions of Dante, Bernard of Clairvaux, Donne, Herbert, Milton, Hopkins, Eliot, R.S. Thomas, and Denise Levertov—down to the poet whose work is in your hand. With the selection of this volume you are entering this enduring tradition, and as a reader contributing to it.

—D.S. Martin
Series Editor

Collections in this series include:

Six Sundays toward a Seventh
by Sydney Lea

Epitaphs for the Journey
by Paul Mariani

Within This Tree of Bones
by Robert Siegel

Particular Scandals
by Julie L. Moore

Gold
by Barbara Crooker

A Word In My Mouth
by Robert Cording

Scape
by Luci Shaw

Conspiracy of Light
by D. S. Martin (forthcoming)

Say This Prayer into the Past

poems

PAUL J. WILLIS

CASCADE *Books* • Eugene, Oregon

SAY THIS PRAYER INTO THE PAST
Poems

Copyright © 2014 Paul J. Willis. All rights reserved. Except for brief quotations in critical publications or reviews, no part of this book may be reproduced in any manner without prior written permission from the publisher. Write: Permissions, Wipf and Stock Publishers, 199 W. 8th Ave., Suite 3, Eugene, OR 97401.

Cascade Books
An Imprint of Wipf and Stock Publishers
199 W. 8th Ave., Suite 3
Eugene, OR 97401

www.wipfandstock.com

ISBN 13: 978-1-62564-167-0

Cataloging-in-Publication data:

Willis, Paul J., 1955–.

> Say this prayer into the past / Paul J. Willis.

> p.; 23 cm—Includes bibliographical references and index.

> ISBN 13: 978-1-62564-167-0

> 1. 2. 3. 4. I. II.

CALL NUMBER 2014

Manufactured in the USA.

*For Kristin and Levi
and all the rest—
you know who you are*

*. . . that I may know how to sustain
the weary with a word.*
—Isaiah 50:4

Table of Contents

Acknowledgments | xiii

Free Verse | 1

I. Cousin Quartet | 3
What Then I Was | 5
Flood | 6
Family Systems | 7
As an Athlete Dying Young | 9
My Son, My Son | 10
Christmas Child | 11
Piano | 12
Gift | 13
February | 14
San Ysidro Canyon | 15
When We First Told You | 16
Cousin Quartet | 17
Seconds | 18
Turning Fifty | 19
Burn Victims | 20
Pausing Out Front | 21

II. Understory | 23
Baker Creek Campground | 25
Almost Spring at the Hut | 26
Hoh River Road | 27
Skunk Cabbage | 28

Table of Contents

Mariposa Grove | 29
Understory | 30
Curlieu Falls | 31
Red Rock Falls | 32
Atwell Bridge | 33
Bubbs Creek | 34
Sunrise in Humphreys Basin | 35
Mountain Hemlock | 36
A Likeness | 37
Midsummer | 38
White Chief Canyon | 39
Mule Ears | 40
Barney Lake Trail | 41
Proposal in a Modest Meadow | 42
Rock Island Lake | 43
Dusy Basin | 44
After Descending from Buck Creek Pass to a Campsite
    on the Chiwawa River | 45
Puerto Vallarta Mountaineer | 46
Los Prietos | 47
Listen | 48
Bearpaw Meadow | 49
Mt. Gould | 50
Late October, Mineral King | 51
Oso Creek | 52
Yuba | 53

III. Green Studies | 55

Peer Editing in Santa Barbara | 57
Green Studies | 58
Grammar Quiz | 59
ROTC, 1974 | 60
Only a Robin | 61
A Lovely Girl | 62
Making Trail | 63
Duck Pond | 64
Saturday Hike | 65
Speaker Phone | 66

Table of Contents

Picture on a Study Wall | 67
Juneau Icefield, 1973 | 69
Little Ruaha River, 1998 | 70
Croquet at Hengrave, 1992 | 71
Teacher | 72
Intercession | 73
The Visitor from Hollywood Reports on Her Day Job | 74
Assessment | 75
The Consultant | 76
Graduation | 77
Homecoming | 78
Necessities | 79
Lost and Found | 80

IV. Antediluvian Baseball | 81

Going Down in History | 83
Antediluvian Baseball | 84
Dido | 85
Art Is a Fire | 86
Upon Avon | 87
The Fair Ophelia Hesitates on the Trinity River | 88
Elizabeth Barrett Contemplates the *Sonnets from the Portuguese* | 89
A Wish | 91
Dinah Morris Digresses in Her Evening Sermon on the Green | 92
David Douglas Writes Home Concerning
    the California Mission Fathers, 1832 | 93
Colin Campbell Cooper | 94
First Rain | 95
FDNY | 96
On the 225th Year of Mission Santa Barbara | 98

Notes | 99

Acknowledgments

I wish to thank the editors of the following publications, in which some of these poems first appeared:

Acorn: "A Likeness" and "Yuba"
Artlife: "Rock Island Lake"
Askew: "Barney Lake Trail," "Croquet at Hengrave," "Homecoming," "Little Ruaha River," "Midsummer," "Mt. Gould," "Only a Robin" (as "Recall"), and "Peer Editing in Santa Barbara" (as "Peer Editing")
Beyond the Valley of the Contemporary Poets (Valley Contemporary Poets): "Almost Spring at the Hut"
California State Poetry Quarterly: "Flood"
Christian Century: "Cousin Quartet," "Green Studies," "Intercession," "Listen," "Necessities," "Skunk Cabbage," and "When We First Told You"
Christianity and Literature: "Elizabeth Barrett Contemplates the *Sonnets from the Portuguese*"
Cider Press Review: "Gift"
Climbing Art: "San Ysidro Canyon"
Cotyledon: "Mule Ears"
Cresset: "Late October, Mineral King" and "Making Trail"
Ekphrasis: "Dido"
English Journal: "Assessment" and "Grammar Quiz"
An Even Dozen (Sullivan Goss): "Colin Campbell Cooper"
From Glory to Glory (Poetry in the Cathedral): "Mountain Hemlock" and "On the 225th Year of Mission Santa Barbara"
Iambs & Trochees: "Turning Fifty"
Interdisciplinary Studies in Literature and the Environment: "Dusy Basin"
Kerf: "David Douglas Writes Home Concerning the California Mission Fathers," "Saturday Hike," and "Sunrise in Humphreys Basin"

Acknowledgments

Kinesis: "Graduation"
Lamp-Post: "Christmas Child"
Manzanita: "Picture on a Study Wall"
New Song: "Bubbs Creek"
Other Journal: "Bearpaw Meadow"
Perspectives: "Burn Victims"
Phase and Cycle: "As an Athlete Dying Young" and "What Then I Was"
Poetry Depth Quarterly: "Going Down in History"
Radix: "Piano"
Relief: "Dinah Morris Digresses in Her Evening Sermon on the Green"
A Ritual to Read to Each Other: Poems in Conversation with William Stafford (Woodley Press): "Los Prietos"
Rock & Sling: "Duck Pond"
Rolling Coulter: "The Consultant" and "February"
Ruminate: "Baker Creek Campground," "Mariposa Grove," and "Red Rock Falls"
Santa Barbara Independent: "My Son, My Son"
Santa Barbara Review: "Oso Creek"
Slant: "The Visitor from Hollywood Reports on Her Day Job"
Solo Novo: "ROTC, 1974" and "White Chief Canyon"
So Luminous the Wildflowers: An Anthology of California Poets (Tebot Bach): "First Rain"
SPMS&H: "Upon Avon"
Stonework: "Curlieu Falls"
Troubadour: "A Lovely Girl"
Tucumcari Literary Review: "A Wish"
Weber: The Contemporary West: "After Descending from Buck Creek Pass to a Campsite on the Chiwawa River" and "Puerto Vallarta Mountaineer"
Westmont: "Art Is a Fire" and "FDNY"
Where Icarus Falls (Santa Barbara Review Publications): "Antediluvian Baseball"
Windhover: "Seconds"

"Gift" has also appeared in *The Bubble*.
"On the 225th Year of Mission Santa Barbara" has also appeared in *The Broadsider* (Poor Souls Press).
"Piano" has also appeared in *A Christmas Collection* (July Literary Press).

Free Verse

I went down to the stream to fish for a poem.
It finned under the lee side of a mossy boulder,
not about to venture out for anything so obvious
as an iamb. I tried a silver anapest, then a
flashy hendecasyllabic lure. Nothing doing.

Then I attached the promise of a prize
in the *Southern Review*. Honorable mention—
that old, rusty, barbless hook. No luck.

The borrowed effusion of salmon eggs
came next, but they got snagged
on somebody else's line. So I clamped
on a lead-shot sinker or two with my back molars
and let the native earthworm—the one I had found
beneath the rotting bark of my conscience—
writhe to the bottom of the pool.

The poem darted out from the rock and took
the worm, the hook, the reel.
I felt it quivering in my creel—
then let it go, into this wild and babbling book.

I. Cousin Quartet

What Then I Was

The first moments of waking this morning
I was a boy, wanting my mother and father
to be getting dressed in the next room.

Mom would limp ahead to the kitchen,
Dad would stay in his undershirt
and lather up a close shave.

Boxes of cereal would appear, rhubarb,
a man with a tie. We would sit down
to the radio news, the whole world

could be neatly blamed on JFK.
I wanted it all over again, that time
before the assassination of childhood.

In those moments of waking
I did not bleed, there were no thorns,
the intimations were clear and full.

I was all the way across the room
before I came to my latter self,
for a while I was very safe.

Flood

Fog rises now from the rainsoaked land,
floating the heavy hills behind. Lawn
gives way. The birds don't mind,
clearing the air on sodden wings.

They saw me sink my van to the doors,
creature of habit, having to get
to work on time. I jumped from the car
and pushed the pickup of a stranger
out of the creek, straining against the mud,
the current, thinking a little of my mother,
nine years old, carried
in the arms of my grandpa
waist-deep in the orange grove.

Just yesterday the beach was lined
with avocados, tumbling out of the brown surf.
Before the grove my people came far
over the sea to this dry place of fruit and stone.
We are still crossing the waters together.

Family Systems

My great-grandmother gave to her minister husband
a baby daughter, then watched him die of typhoid.
This was in Denver. Next she married a circuit-riding
Methodist and gave three daughters more.

In Oklahoma City the rider founded a home
for fallen women, and she accused him every night
of helping them to fall further. Then she left
with all four daughters for Fort Worth and married again.

Her oldest ran away from home to work
as a manicurist in hotels in Brownsville, Wichita.
Some said she did more than that. Before she reached
the age of twenty, she took a dose of arsenic,

just like Madame Bovary, and spent the last hour
of her wretched life in a screaming match
with my great-grandmother. In my family,
that hour has never stopped happening.

Then my great-grandmother took the daughters
she had left and rode the train to Los Angeles,
where she disapproved of each young man
her daughters married. So the men vanished—

along with her third husband, whom she accused
of shacking up with one daughter or the other.
After that, an elderly gentleman picked her up
in his automobile once a week in the afternoon

and brought her home in the evening.
I do not think she loved this man, for she
refused to speak of him. When my young mother,
an innocent girl from an orange grove, was putting the final

touches on her bridal veil, my great-grandmother
marched into the dressing room and said,
"I'll give you six months." I'll say this for her, though.
During the war, the Hayashida family that ran the cleaners

next door was put in a stall at the Santa Anita race track.
My great-grandmother took a trolley to the track
and gave the commanding officer a piece of her mind.
I am very sure she gave to him a piece of her mind.

As an Athlete Dying Young

When they took you off the breathing
tube you were rasping hard, as if
you had finished a sprint, a mile,
a marathon, your eyes squeezed
shut, not ready to see your time.

Your sisters beat you, Ruth and Ethel
by a split decade or so, Carrie by almost
eighty years, wind-aided with arsenic.

You, Ida, are the last to find
your parents reconciled with wreaths
of shade. The family is complete
again, together now, a record
written on the world in breathlessness.

My Son, My Son

Since I saw your grandpa die
I like to watch you breathe.

Mornings especially,
to see the air move easily

across your lip hung down in slumber,
poised to waken, ripen, bleed.

I like to watch the rise and fall
of chest within your soft blue sleeper,

already muscled round like his,
ready to heave new cords of oak

and pick up untold heaviness
where he left off.

I like to watch your eyes unclose
the confused but steady luster of dawn,

clear skies born from gasp of night,
the breathless story.

Christmas Child

When you were born, sycamore leaves
were brown and falling. They sifted
through the stable door and laid their hands
upon your cheek. Sunlight bent
through cracks in the wall and found
your lips. It was morning now.
Joseph slept, curled on the straw in a corner.

Your mother offered her breast
to you, the warm milk of humankind,
of kindness. You drank from the spongy
flesh as you could, a long way now
from vinegar, but closer, closer,
closer than the night before.

She cradles you, O Jesus Christ,
born in blood and born to bleed,
for this brief dawn a simple child, searching
the nipple, stirring among the whisper,
the touch, of sycamore.

Piano

The summer you were seven
you could hardly sleep
that night before your first recital.
"I'd rather break my arm," you said.

Which is what you did with an hour
to spare. We could blame the dog
who chased you into the glass door,
but that would be dumb. A wish,

you found, is a dangerous thing.
Today, eight years old and nearly
Christmas, you asked to be the first
on the program. As you sat waiting,

sunlight fell on the bowl-cut line
behind your head. Sometimes
just a year is enough to learn
to bring joy to the world.

Gift

after Barry Spacks

You bring me a chartreuse tennis ball,
dropped at my feet and shining
with the wetness of your enormous tongue,
which lolls now from the side of your mouth
like a slice of baloney slipping
out of a sandwich made of
mayonnaise and Wonder Bread.

The weight of the ball in my hand!
Its arc in the sky!
The way it leaves the inside
of my every finger suffused and slick
with the most intimate taste of you.
The way, when your hurrying back is turned,
there is time to wipe them clean on the grass.

February

This is the season of sourgrass,
shy, lovely, beside the driveway.
Hanna gathers the stalks in her arms
like so many sheaves of daffodils
across her shoulder, green, gold.

I remember the alley behind
my grandmother's house in Anaheim,
rifted with them along the fence.
One by one I crushed their stems
across my teeth, dripping the delight
of winter down my lips. A shudder,
an ache, in the roots of my tongue,
the approaching impossibility
of too much good in the world.

San Ysidro Canyon

Yesterday my daughter slipped
from underneath an overhang
some sixty feet above the ground.
She had climbed so sure and ably
to that hold. I squeezed the rope
and stopped her almost casually,
bolts and slings and carabiners
doing their allotted work.

There was one second no not even
part of one when all nine years
went hurtling down and all the threads
between us snapped to mute attention:
she so high and helpless, I
still grasping for her far below,
fingers cold and filled with
a cord not easily broken.

When We First Told You

Gail, remember the boy that broke
his neck on the campus lawn—
just kidding around, turning flips
with his college buddies?
He got his diploma this afternoon
with a standing ovation that had to end.

When we first told you about this boy,
your face turned lost, you thought
of your own at twenty-one,
somersaulted into a field by a Mack truck.

That was a moment I could love you,
though sons-in-law are poor in love.
That was a moment love lay
languishing before you, bleeding
from a crown of thorns
and once more giving up your ghost.

Cousin Quartet

Years ago, my mother sang in a quartet
with her sister Lorraine and their two cousins.
The Cousin Quartet, it was called.
I just asked her about it tonight, as she lay dying.

"The funny thing was," she said,
"we always stood with our backs to a window.
And someone was always pouring sand."

I asked my aunt about these things;
she shook her head. And so we gather
evidence for the fading music
of the mind, the light behind us.
And someone is always pouring sand.

Seconds

No, not first love, and not love at first sight,
but friends who've come to love and to take care
of one another until death do slight
another time, whenever time shall wear.
There's mystery when two become one pair,
when darkness that is grieving turns to light;
there's hope within the common sense we share,
a turning to each other in the night.

Thus do we gather to make old vows new,
acknowledging a marriage of true minds
and truer hearts, if human hearts be true.
Love is not love which lessens when it finds
a second love. And so we witness this:
a holy hesitation, and a kiss.

Turning Fifty

It's not so bad, they say. It's not so old:
no difference at all from forty-nine.
But now that I am here, the country looks
foreshortened up ahead and vast behind,
blank reaches on the map of memory.

I think of mountain ranges row on row
that fade into the air, once crossed and climbed
but now too far away to re-ascend.
That's why I had my party on a peak
behind the town I live in. From the top,

small knots of pilgrims could be seen below
on threads of trail in the chaparral.
They were my former selves, all come to pay
their courtesies, to greet this relic soul,
to see what might be left to recognize.

Burn Victims

The oak trees by the creek are sweating blood.
There where the fire passed through, pressed by the wind,
their barks are blackened, and oozing through the singe,
red beads of sap drip sorrowingly down
to ashes. If we knew Gethsemane
were not a garden anymore and wept
itself, the knotty foreheads of each burl
contracted in one brow of woe, our prayer
would not be for life's cup but merely that
our hearts might burn within us. Seared and scarred,
we'd bleed in hope of olives buried deep
among the roots, where what remains may rise.

Pausing Out Front

Someone else lives here now, Cadillac in the garage,
chicken wire stretched across the wrought-iron fence
to cage a poodle prancing through the open door.

It does not bark. White rocking chairs
salute a dangled flag on the porch.
That is where our son sat through the passing light of afternoons
to marvel at the quiet pace of his own breathing,
our frayed retriever at his feet.

Behind that porch I rested on a cool, dark couch
and wondered what was left of us, now that our old house
on the hill had vanished in a night of flame.

In the kitchen, you lifted plates and silverware
that were strangely heavy in your hand.
And in the darkened living room our daughter
sat with a cautious suitor who settled in like a rain of ashes.

This shady little home downtown,
somnolent beside the buzz of motorcycles
on the street—it was a refuge,
a hospice or a hospital we scarcely knew.

Some of us got better there, some got worse,
but we lay our heads in gratitude in that dim place,
in that year of shadow, and today as I shift
my feet on the curb, peering through the open door,
I say this prayer into the past, I nod my thanks.

II. Understory

Baker Creek Campground

Warm tonight for February. The creek flows
under bare and moonlit cottonwoods,
and the Owens Valley spreads below
as if it belongs. Once in a while, distant
headlights find us from the other side.

Miles across that winter range
are cones and dishes aimed into space,
listening for life on other planets.
That's what a friend told me—a government
project—and I haven't known him to lie.

Another friend, a girl that I knew in college,
once made a climb on New Year's Eve
to a lake behind us in the Sierra. It was frozen
shut, and the winds had swept the snow aside.

Under the stars, her companions whirled her
back and forth across the ice like a broom ball,
and she let out a scream that thirty years later
the government still can't hear. She said
she would remember that. I would.

Almost Spring at the Hut

The front porch of Ostrander, a murmur
of voices from inside the wooden door,
new sun piercing your side, the cirque
entangled with ski tracks lovely
in their braided curves, and the granite
hoof of Horse Ridge pawing a pale
sliver of moon.   Silence is here,
where stars spoke their many, many
selves in the night. The croak
of a raven in red fir, that is all, and blue
and blue of sky that quiets interruption.

—*Yosemite National Park*

Hoh River Road

Just up from the Hard Rain Café,
among bare, wet alders and dripping cedars,
a lovely girl is folding sweaters
in an empty mountain shop.

My handsome son and I stop in
for aspirin on our way to a hike,
but he is the one with the headache
and I am the one who is clearly smitten.

So happy to see us, she says, and blushes,
looking happy to see my son in particular.
Where are we from? She has never
been south of Oakland, she says—
too dry for her skin. She touches her cheek.

A poster over the door displays
a girl climbing a granite wall
in sunshine, her sling of gear
grazing the rock beneath her shoulders.
The same dark hair. The same dark eyes.

So I inquire. She touches her cheek.
We're not the first to ask, she says.
But no, she says. If only, she says.
We take the aspirin from her hand

and exit into the hard rain, leaving
the girl to fold her sweaters
in the dryness of the shop,
the precious dryness under the eaves.

—*Olympic National Park*

Skunk Cabbage

I've seen it in the hollows of the Cascades in Oregon,
    and head-high on the trail from Juneau up to the Icefield,
there to perplex
    the pink mouth of a black bear.

And here it is along Cedar Creek in Michigan—
    dark green, leafy as ever,
moisting out of the dark ravines
    like misplaced dollar bills.

But what can you buy this time of year
    with skunk cabbage?
Just this: violet, trillium, marigold,
    spring beauty.

Mariposa Grove

Wet meadow in deep woods.
On the edges, grass combed brown and flat
by the heavy hand of snow.

But greening up in the center—
moss, shoots, water trickling
through the muck.

A sequoia log dams the flow,
holds it richly, pooling hope
beneath the faith of fluted giants,

ragged crowns. Thick roots reach
and reach, gather what remains unseen,
terra infirma, this sodden stage

of ferns, of fungus, marigolds.

—*Yosemite National Park*

Understory

(*Cornus nuttallii*)

Dogwood blossoms mount into the sunshine
   as if they were creators of light,
     as if the air were only blue

because of them, as if the pale
   cinnamon of sequoia bark were like
     the moon, a borrowed glow.

If understory, the story under
   all things else, stair-stepping
     into sky like angels on a green-leafed ladder.

There, *there*, and even *there*—
   as friend with friend, taking us upward,
     in heaven as it is on earth.

—*Sequoia National Park*

Curlieu Falls

Mid-May in the Sierra—
this is when the water knows
to fling itself

from cliffs and ledges,
spray through chartreuse
alder leaves.

Then it curls in granite
channels, licking the moss,
and calms the shade

below the live oak terraces,
the bleeding heart, the nodding
heads of saxifrage.

—*Sierra National Forest*

Red Rock Falls

The waters come curling over
the mottled granite, combed
by a log that is wet and heavy with decay.

Azalea, alder, hazelnut
hang over the plunge pool, green
upon green, and the creamy
blossoms of dogwood mount up
like clear stars in the afternoon.

If I knew of a reason to leave,
I might. The white fir, almost black
against the brightness of the sky.

—Sierra National Forest

Atwell Bridge

The river washes its sudden way
through stone channels,
polishing its history.

A sequoia watches
the water passing, green
pools rippling below.

The white fir and sugar pine
that shoulder up
are new arrivals.

Even newer the wooden bridge
across this shade.

And I, this morning,
newest of all.

Except, it seems
I have been here before.

The wood fern nod.
Yes, they say, *you have been
here for a long time.*

—*Sequoia National Park*

Bubbs Creek

Hey, Bubb. It's good to see you after twenty years.
We hiked you on our honeymoon—it's been that long.
I'm glad to report we are still married, just as it seems
that you are to these granite shelves, this water ouzel,

those lodgepole pine along your banks, their scratchy
bark so different from your cool, smooth surface
in the meadows. Not that you're so easy to live with.
Now as then, you say in your whitewater roar,

Don't cross me. And I rarely do.
How else could you run swift and wild, each turn
a new clear pool or fall of infinite variety
within the spacious limits of your chosen course?

What you touch comes green with life: willows,
grasses, stone-drenched mosses—even this morning,
at first light, row on row of shooting stars,
deep purple with tomorrow's joy.

–Kings Canyon National Park

Sunrise in Humphreys Basin

Light beating the suncups,
those rippled seas. Water
falling from icy tarns,
peaks waking, golden granite
capped with egg-white cornices.

From here the light slips down
and down, couloir to canyon,
whitebark, lodgepole.
In the meadow far below,
a lake of shadow, disappearing.

—*John Muir Wilderness*

Mountain Hemlock

(Tsuga mertensiana)

Bent under snowpack
at timberline, wait for release.

At summer solstice, spring
into sharp air, shed and fling
the ice clods from supple branches.

Half-stooped
from nine months in little room,
make your bows to the world.

A Likeness

(*Quercus agrifolia*)

Live oaks and elephants, the gray
curled skin, hard-shifting shanks
and knees. These trees

never forget what they take
from earth, what they give back.
Birds land on their heads all day

and bask in sky till fog
rolls in. Then thick feet lumber
and stand while darkness falls,

trunks lifted up to the moon.

Midsummer

This evening we are awash in light.
   It buoys the mountains as if they have finally
      found their proper medium, their true home,

as if only now the peaks and ridges
   and chaparral have come to the surface
      and are free to look around, to take in air,
         to catch us up in their respiration.

If only we could bathe ourselves
   in light like this the whole year through.
      Could we survive, amidst so much joy?

This evening is the highest tide,
   the crest of possibility.
      All ships come in:
         hulls sleek, sails shining.

White Chief Canyon

A steep climb to the crushed cabin,
rusty litter of mining tools
under the trees, and the creek
in the pasture is rocky and dry.

But corn lily grows
lush like a lost patch of a lone pioneer,
and silver trunks lie pitched
across the sunburnt grass

under the bare flanks of granite,
a reminder of avalanches that come,
like the one set off in 1906
by the earthquake in San Francisco,

or the one in the winter of '69,
enough to discourage Walt Disney
from building a restaurant
and ski lift here, while I sit

alone with the lodgepole pine
on the verge
of this breeze-freshened meadow,
grateful for every place that is wild.

—*Sequoia National Park*

Mule Ears

(Wyethia mollis)

Mule ears, mule ears, listening
to the squeak of the ground squirrel,
wind sends soul to you,
wavering, the stubborn yellow
of your blossom.

Barney Lake Trail

Jeffrey pine hold out their arms
where we begin. They drop their cones
whenever they are good and ready—
and we kick them aside with a little dance.

The creek is still here,
and the aspen too, all in a flutter,
nervous about company.

When we bed down for the night,
the stars will watch, and so will the bears.

They will say to each other, *These people.*

—Hoover Wilderness

Proposal in a Modest Meadow

Monkeyflower crowds the foot of a waterfall
(those buttercup faces, up to something),

and a dipper flies the bends of the creek
down to a veil of mountain hemlock.

Overhead, granite climbs
to its appointed place in the sky.

Once, above that mountaintop,
a red-tailed hawk nested itself in pure air,

its feathers flapping on the wind
like a flag of no nation I know.

—*Hoover Wilderness*

Rock Island Lake

Just over the heather divide,
fields of lupine
sweep down an open shore.

The air holds
light and breath and beauty,
drinkable like falling water.

By granite boulders,
three pools of obsidian flakes,
their black shine.

—*Yosemite National Park*

Dusy Basin

We open our eyes on a crescent moon at dawn
over the Palisades. Below our heads, the quiet
outlet of the lake repeats itself, and yellow-legged

frogs hide in the small current. The lake is still
still where we watched a bear swim clean across
in the silence of the evening. The rocky islands

are still as frogs, as the eyes and heads of waiting
frogs. The whitebark pine that hide the cache
of those who came to count the frogs are dark

and still upon sleeping slabs, upon tawny grass
remembering the green of day. Above the browning
silhouette of Agassiz, Winchell, Thunderbolt,

of Isosceles and Columbine, the moon
lies tipped on its back, ready to receive
the morning into its wide and slender arms.

–Kings Canyon National Park

After Descending from Buck Creek Pass
to a Campsite on the Chiwawa River

As much as we long for a swimming hole,
none appears. The rapids course
under crowded banks of alder, bracken, devil's club.
Beneath the boulders in the current,
bedrock: the marbled bones of the North Cascades.

We nest in the forest of grand fir
among rotting logs, the delicate
petals of queen's cup. There in the night
we lie half-drifting in the duff,
the sound of rivers in our ears.

—*Glacier Peak Wilderness*

Puerto Vallarta Mountaineer

He climbs the palm in the way you might
prusik out of a deep crevasse
you have fallen into by mistake,

except the rope to which he attaches
the knotted cords is the corrugated
trunk of this tree. Once in the crown,

he does not collapse with gratitude
on the snowy lip, for here begins
his real work, stroking away

at the clusters of green coconuts
as if bringing his ice ax firmly to bear
on the blue shear of the next serac.

When lowering the hewn clusters
to the sand, he parks his machete
with just a touch in the arm of a frond

as if he has reached the next belay.
From where he rests, he feels the wind
through ocean passes, hears the waves

of braided streams, then descends
like a glacier melting down
to dust on the forest floor.

Los Prietos

The yucca fans ascend the folded
sandstone cliffs like rows of sea anemones,
memory of when these layers accrued
upon an ocean floor. Funny how the earth
is given to recapitulation, how our own race
repeats itself. I, for example, sitting on this gravel
shore at a long and silent bend in the river,
watching the willow yellow
where it has gone sere and sere before,
thinking about the men who bathed in this deep pool
after a day of building trail, far from the reddening
paths of war, I too a prisoner of spiny conscience,
leaving sediments of self upon this bank,
layer upon folded layer.

—*Los Padres National Forest*

Listen

A lake lies all alone in its own shape.
It's not going anywhere.

A lake can wait a long time
for a hiker to come
and camp on its shore.

It will reflect the moonlight,
give him a drink of pale silver.

Toward dawn, the wind might ruffle
it a little, and the water
will have words with the granite.

Once the hiker goes away
through October meadows,

the lake will sparkle by itself.
You'll never see it. There is
so much you will never see.

Bearpaw Meadow

Incense cedar, elderberry,
scattered chapels of white fir.
Cones stand up like paper squirrels

on the branches, waxing
resinous in sun—light of the year
yet lingering with warmth in plenty,

here, now, an afternoon
in folded grass and browning nests
of bracken under broken

granite, lucid sky. Stillness
after ache and heave
of summer, no one here beside,

and no one thinking of the snow.

—*Sequoia National Park*

Mt. Gould

What does it mean to reach a summit
    rimmed and skiffed with October snow?
        We sit on a terrace and pass around

the register to hold our names. On the descent,
    our shadows cross the paling granite, leave
        the sun to warm the places we held on.

There is a memory, of course, of edges
    on our fingertips, a lingering ache
        within our knees. But still, for what?

There are places where earth meets the sky,
    and we go to them to meet each other
        and ourselves. *Yes*, we shall say,

we climbed that—forgetful of
    the snow, the air, the stone
        that climbed inside of us.

–*John Muir Wilderness*

Late October, Mineral King

It is the kind of afternoon in which
shade and sun please equally.
Smoke-filled valleys pale below,
but we climb into bluer skies
on remnant snow in the ravines.

How does the trail know where
to turn? Why do the wood grouse
wait for us around the bend?
What makes each pair of trees we pass
a new door, an old welcome?

—Sequoia National Park

Oso Creek

November light in the sycamore leaves,
one faint suggestion of autumn
in this part of California, the green
and brown illuminated from within,
saying self and saying sight upon the canyon
underneath where stream finds pool
and pool. Boulders shade the outcome
of leaf and water, ready to receive remains
of sodden life, newmade earth
the darkness and the memory of year again.

−*Los Padres National Forest*

Yuba

This grassy terrace above mossed cliffs
is all we need, given our feet
and December sun.

The trail leads upward
under the oaks,
into the snow breeze from the Sierra—

winter kiss
in the green-pooled canyons.

III. Green Studies

Peer Editing in Santa Barbara

Some of the students bunch together,
desks turned inward. A few reluctant souls
lean back, chairs set apart and askew.

One boy hovers between two clusters—
assigned to one, inclined to another.
Inclined, in fact, toward a dusky blonde.

The boy writes all of his papers
on what he has learned as a president
of the Future Farmers of America;

the dusky blonde writes about
an almond grove in the San Joaquin.
Three years later, her second-graders

will send me crayon tracings of turkeys
when I lose my house to a fire
just before Thanksgiving.

By then, the boy will be back
on his tractor, leaving a cloud of dust
like smoke alongside Highway 99.

But now, in this eternal present,
Montecito, lush and lazy, sleeps
outside the classroom window.

His desk, her desk, are almost
touching in the green shadows of light,
almost on the same page.

Green Studies

I like the way that shrubs and flowers
lean against my classroom windows
as if wanting to enroll. What would the azalea
say when asked about the Forest of Arden?
And would the red, red rose respond
to my mistress' eyes as something,
after all, like the sun? What's not to like
in these my vernal, budding pupils—
so firmly rooted in this soil, so curiously
intertwined? My vegetable love should grow
with each new bell of earnest fragrance,
fair and passing fair, each one.
As Eve once more eats of that fruit,
I hear their universal groan.

Grammar Quiz

The boy who is nearly blind
brings one large eye to the page,
bending down, forehead to desk,
as if taking a needed nap.

But he is searching furiously
for colons and commas that float
like paragliders in and out
of the peaks of print.

The other students have already
landed in the meadow, where they
are starting to think about supper
at a Mexican place, the fresh

guacamole this time of year.
The blind boy, nose to the sandstone,
is still spread-eagled on the summit.
The night there will be very cold.

ROTC, 1974

The day that I wore red white & blue
boxer shorts to morning drill,
Major Winslow rushed into my face
with a clipboard. "Your name, cadet!"

It was winter, and my legs shone pale
in regulation black shoes and black socks.
"Hanger," I told him. "Cliff Hanger."
He wrote it down as if his pen
were assassinating each false letter,
and then he dismissed me,
me and my troop of followers
in colored shirts and bow ties.

That night, a Texas boy from across the hall
came through my door and slid
his arm around my shoulders.
"You know," he said, "men have died
in that uniform." "You know," I said,
"more men have died in their boxer shorts."

Only a Robin

Yes, but it sends over the passing trucks
    a kind of song, Midwestern, that I have not heard

since college in the early mornings, waking
    early in Illinois, thinking of the way that ivy

lightens in the latticed window, how dew
    quiets the nearest lawn, how I might climb

the chapel roof and see where prairie
    must have spread its aria, its passing wings.

A Lovely Girl

There is a girl reading on the lawn.
Last week a cypress tree fell where she lies.
Now there is grass, and peace—the tree is gone.
And there's a girl reading on the lawn.

The sky is blue, a football sails on,
and higher up hang-gliders stoop and rise;
there's one I know that landed after dawn
and dented in a roof and broke his brawn.

But there's a girl reading on the lawn.
And neither trees nor young men from the skies
nor footballs dropping past can put upon
a lovely girl reading on the lawn.

Making Trail

At first, he raked a few eucalyptus limbs
and leaves from the face of the ground, cut
down some poison oak. But soon
he had shoveled a dirt path up every canyon
of the campus, laid out switchbacks
on the hills, connected stream to stream
until a secret web contained us all.

It kept growing. He found himself asking
the college president if she wouldn't mind
the occasional hiker just below her patio.
And he thought about the Winchester House
in San Jose, the woman who added room
to room, built stairways into empty space.

Why is it when we start something, we cannot stop?
Cheops and his pyramid, rails to Omaha—
trenches on the Somme, perhaps. Or, on a sunny
afternoon, just tinkering around with an atom.

Lately he has been pondering the luster of soil,
the shape and scent of it, winding across the cranberry
carpet of the faculty lounge. How it would meander
like the flaking crest of a gopher's passage,
taking the eye out the door, into the distance.

Duck Pond

The fountain comes mouthing
out of an earthen pot that is slick with moss and tilted

on a sandstone outcrop in the middle.
The water spurts modestly, as if from the lips

of a playful swimmer on his back,
then recalls itself to the pool,

a scattering that spreads in rings
until they touch the planted feet of Pharaoh's

daughter disrobing to bathe—
except she has found a baby

in a basket of ferns
and reaches her alabaster arms,

as surprised as I am now to see a pair of mallards
resting in the lily pads, a small green turtle

climbing onto another outcrop, arching its neck
as if to gain a better view of November light.

Saturday Hike

Beer cans on a sandstone outcrop
hidden in the chaparral: this foggy morning,
the party's over. I load them into my rucksack,
where they clank and leak their sweet and sour
across my spine. Brightening in sun
below, the tasteful mansions of Montecito
turn their backs upon the hills and face
their porticoes to sea. From a bend
in the trail, I can see a tiny man
on his flagstone driveway, drinking the news
from a cell phone in his empty hand.

Speaker Phone

The candidate we interview is kept
within a plastic presence on the table.
It's gray, a four-armed octopus, if such
exist in some debilitated form.
Her voice comes bubbling to our ears as from
the deep—green waves of static interrupt—
and we reply as calling from the deck
of some lost fishing boat in nameless straits.
The table pitches, yaws, the creature slides
from end to end before its tentacles
attach their suckers to the helpless chair.
He drowns in his reply; we clutch the mast,
our voices waving to us from the vast.

Picture on a Study Wall

I glance up from my books to Sawtooth Ridge,
the northeast boundary of Yosemite,
still backlit by a storm. Beneath the clouds
the shattered granite falls in fins and shrouds
into a wasted glacier on the left;
dull ice and talus mark a year of drought,
the summer of the bicentennial.
That year I came of age. I must have stood
on Cleaver Peak to take this photograph:
the ridge escapes before. In sunlight first,
the Sawblade. I once climbed it by mistake—
off-route, off-peak—and found its highest jag
at sunset after long approach, belays
interminable, followed by a set
of blind rappels down to the dusky snow.
Three Teeth are next, the western one a cube
of rock perched on a summit pedestal.
For two whole hours we tried to find a way
the final thirty feet—and never did.
Then comes the Doodad, wildly overhung,
but yielding a crack we often stemmed.
To that strange rooftop all the meadows of
Slide Canyon offer invitation
to ease back down to lupine, lakes, and groves.
And we accepted, every time, with thanks.
The massy Dragtooth fills the further sky,
thick buttresses that claw their way to earth.
The north face beckons, as it always has—
six pitches, dark and glistening and firm.
The holds are sure, and say, as does John Muir,
Who wouldn't be a mountaineer! Beyond
and partly hidden where the clouds turn white,
the Matterhorn (old muse of dharma bums),
from this side much more like the Parthenon,

one columned crest. It is a temple we
once slept upon, and to that summit comes
the dawn above the sagebrush in the east,
the granite blushing, stars still thick with cold,
we shivering there, still pale, and not yet old.

Juneau Icefield, 1973

Every other day we crossed the Lemon and the Ptarmigan, following a line of stakes. Each one we measured with a tape to see how far the snow had melted. The Lemon grew, the Ptarmigan shrank. Why the difference? No one knew. These glaciers shared a common ridge that overlooked the ocean channel, long day's hike down steep meadow, rain forest. At times the trail disappeared in fern head-high, the skunk cabbage lapped at your chest. Up on the rocky divide, Quonset huts held off the seething wind and fog while we trudged out to mark our inches, centimeters, resetting when the stakes were high, carefully wedging the wood into the snow or firn as if rooting it there, as if planting our hopes in the thaw of the frozen. We sang as we worked to warm the time, choirboy voices, "Sunrise, Sunset," describing our days, describing the measured course of our glaciers. The whistle of marmots, the cackle of ravens, made us refrain. Sometimes fog dissolved to sleet, sometimes to rain, and once or twice it lifted to reveal the wide Pacific out to Glacier Bay, the gleaming shape of Mt. Fairweather, hanging like a star upon the far horizon, fifteen thousand feet above the distant sea—like love, like song, like living and like dying glaciers—its worth unknown, our height just taken.

Little Ruaha River, 1998

Saturday morning, and Shera, the American girl, is gathering pebbles
for her fishbowl. Some she finds just under the brown water, others in
the mudflat shore. She piles the best ones carefully in the cradle of a
shattered snag. On one bank, eucalyptus and acacia and tall yellowing
grass climb back to her house. On the other, a small grove of bamboo,
where a Bantu appears at dawn to milk the stalks for their white, sweet
juice. It ferments in hours—the men in the village are happily drunk
by afternoon. Last month, the river in flood, one boy drowned here
trying to cross. He was a strong swimmer, they say. In midstream,
a branch reaches out of the current, quavering like an outstretched
hand. Up at the farm where Shera lives, her father keeps no guard at
night—proof, they say, of his power in witchcraft. Two small terriers
sleep upon the porch by day, but at nightfall they grow huge as lions,
and find you anywhere in the dark.

Croquet at Hengrave, 1992

Bored, we began to expand the course,
fixing hoops on hills next to the rue and roses
and planting stakes behind the ornamental

shrubs, the weeping fountain.
"This is the cross-country version!" we declared.
The wooden balls flew past our heads

like grapeshot, like revolution, and splintered
against the stone stairs, the marble benches,
the bulwarks of the manor walls.

What was it we wanted? Overthrow
of the alabaster bust of Queen Elizabeth
that glared down from the latticed window,

liberation from English nuns,
assurance that this blue of noon
could represent the sky, the sky.

Teacher

That lonely stool in front of the class—
a blonde-wood lily pad in air.

There you perch like a spotted frog
and croak your trochees, your anapests,
rocking a little, making waves.

With sticky fingers, you clutch
pen and book, cantilever
your pliant elbows under the obliging ferns.

Was it for this you leapt at the chance—
not to sing, but simply to bellow?

Intercession

When I wake in the night and think
of what I might have said in class that day,
I wonder why my life consists

of inarticulate occasions.
No timely word, only belated ones.
Every hour a first draft, and then another.

It makes me want to announce, "Listen!
Listen to what I do not say. Listen
to what it is you cannot say yourselves."

There are sighs and groans,
     just sighs and groans.
Interpret them, dear ones, as you may.

The Visitor from Hollywood Reports on Her Day Job

What I do is make subtitles in Norwegian.
Not easy. Take *The Simpsons*, for example.
So much wordplay—the double meanings
won't come through. But we don't get paid
to do good work. We throw up something
approximate, or even largely inaccurate,
and the supervisor says good enough.

The important thing is to get to the next
episode. That's why I have to write
on the side, take time to revise.
On the job, no one lets me. I miss that.
And poetry more than anything is about
the exact word. When I find it,
then I can go to sleep at night.

Assessment

Ninety-five percent of those who read this poem
will experience a sense of wonder. The other
five percent are wondering how to arrive
at this statistic. For evidence is what is needed.

Otherwise the poem will never gain accreditation,
and no one will want to attend. We could ask
for a show of hands, but some of the readers are related
to the poet, and nothing surprises them anymore.

If the poem is read aloud, carefully trained monitors
could be placed in the audience to count
the number of mouths agape in stupefaction
or in slumber. How many persons are leaning

forward, eager for the next word? This is an angle
our monitors can quietly measure, pulling
from their back pockets a gathering hush
of collapsible wooden protractors.

If all else fails, electrodes may be placed
on the correct lobes of the brain—
or for certain lines, on the genitals.
The results will be graphed on a table of outcomes

in the report that forever after must be stapled
to the body of this poem. Perhaps you have seen
a great blue heron lumbering down a pond for takeoff,
its feet entwined in dripping skeins of lily pads.

The morning sun illuminates the strain of the wings,
the encumbrance of roots and petals
dragging their weight across the dark brown of the water.
The bird never rises. No wonder.

The Consultant

At our faculty lunch he sat by me
and asked where I had done my work.
I named the place and he said
he had been there several times,
then told us he had served as an aide
to Joe McCarthy in '49, which left me
to wonder what shades of red
there might have been in my school colors.
Bob Kennedy was right there with him,
and also the woman that Bobby married.
Joe McCarthy drank too much and bought
him his first beer, underage, and when
Old Joe died our consultant happened
to be in town and, what the hell,
he stayed for the funeral—after all,
an historic event.

                Once in Detroit
he had interviewed a mousy woman
to teach in his night school, went by the name
of Joyce Carol Oates. He subsequently
appeared as a dean in one of her novels,
also in a cocktail party in one short story,
though the character in it by his name
was clearly based on someone else.
Our consultant had many good friends
from the past, some of them gone,
and he spoke them well, how fortunate
they were to have known him.
He cherished himself among the living,
and granted to us a list of being,
a repository of many names
which he consulted to find his own.

Graduation

Of the names I pronounced from the lectern
under the canopy, there were none
so interesting as Santiago E. Matheus Durran-Ballen
(also Economics and Business).

His family, I know, is well
connected in Ecuador. For their sake,
for the sake of my future reception in Quito,
I released the name with quiet élan,

sending it like a flight of doves across
the field, hard into the shock of sun.
"Ah," they will say, sweeping
me into the porticoed twilight,

"you are the charming young professor
who read our Santi's name so well."
Somewhere fountains ring and echo
the truth of privilege, the benefit of sacrifice.

Homecoming

After the wave of flame
had passed, the walls of our home
now erased, I looked into my study
from a place I had not looked before.

Under the desk that was not there,
a file cabinet was glowing,
a drawer of my poems still
glowing, like the quiet

coals of a bonfire on the quad
when the cheerleaders have already
left, and the beer is gone,
and there is still something to say.

Necessities

My house burned down a month ago, so today
I walked to the bookstore and bought myself
a dictionary, a Bible, and a calendar.

What else does one need, really? For Malvolio,
in that dark cell, it was candle, paper, and ink.
That was his sacred trinity by which he could
be sane again—or at least be proven so.

Me, I need to make sure of the meanings
of words, then to invest them with holiness,
and then to know when I might use them
(or *utilize* them, as an administrator would say).

On Monday, February 2, I plan to employ *perspicacious*.
Then, on Easter, *resurrection* is scheduled
for its grand debut. And so on. I'm saving *horror*
for Halloween, and *thanksgiving* for Thanksgiving.

Among poets of old, this was known as *decorum*.
Proper words in proper places. On the anniversary
of the fire, I will simply say, *damn*.

Lost and Found

If there be such a thing as found poems,
might there be lost poems as well?
And a place to find them after someone
turns them in? You would stop by a battered
desk in a corner, and there with your misplaced
set of keys, the scarf you dropped
in the parking lot, the pair of gloves left
in the restaurant, would be those stanzas of blank
verse you had to forsake when the embers
began to fall upon the roof of your house.
There would be the sonnet you sent
to that slender, acned girl from college—
your only copy—the girl that never wrote back.
Even the limerick you made up on the playground—
the one about your sixth-grade teacher
who frowned her way into retirement.
Every word that in Ariosto lands
on the backside of the moon, or in Milton
on that convex, windy shell of the universe,
the most precious, foolish things you have uttered,
would be handed to you by a woman with bright lipstick,
chewing gum and talking on the phone
with her husband, who is late getting off work but needs
to remember to pick up a loaf of whole-wheat bread
and a half gallon of non-fat on the way home.

IV. Antediluvian Baseball

Going Down in History

Two men from Fort Tejon
come sauntering into Jack-in-the-Box
wearing General Grant campaign hats
and blue wool cavalry coats. They order

bacon cheeseburgers and eat them
in a serious nineteenth-century way,
not looking at each other across the table
when they talk; if their eyes meet

it is only in the line of duty. Soon
they must go back to the fort
and defend it from the present day
at all costs.

Antediluvian Baseball

One night, all the bases came to visit
home plate. While frogs croaked
in the outfield they floated in the batter's box
like lily pads, getting a sense
of where it happened.

Two ravens landed on the pitcher's mound
and called for blood. Aluminum bleachers
began to buzz with St. Elmo's fire, ecstatic.

Then the rain came and told secrets
about antediluvian baseball, how Abel
made it all the way in on a sacrifice,
how Noah saved the best pitchers
but left the umpires to drown.

Dido

after Charles Garabedian

You have left me in blue twilight
without a face—as if the closing
of the day had shut my features

as surely as the gray horizon
is shutting the sail of your ship
inside its watery mouth.

I turn to you—what is left of me
turns to you—blank without your eye
to eye, your scent to scent, your

lip to lip inside that cave.
If I had tongue to speak I would
call after you. I would bless

your kingdom come. The night is cold.
Think of me by your new hearthstone:
be warmed by the light of my pyre.

Art Is a Fire

Art is a fire, for it burns the heart;
it is a phoenix from the ashes rising.
So do not think it can be felt in part,
a cheerful blaze upon the hearth, advising
the viewer of some sweet domestic charm.

It is a conflagration on a slope
that sweeps like silent tidal waves, whose harm
we face without a single, embered hope
that we will ever be one whit the same.

Kinkade, you are a liar. We will go
where darkness visible makes Milton's flame,
where David's heat makes Michelangelo
to know the shape of shoulder in the stone.

Art is a pillar of the finest fire;
it leads us into exile, all alone,
where we must sacrifice upon the pyre
our smoldering flesh, the scorched and sooted bone.

Or if it lead us to a desert home,
it leads us where we do not wish to stray,
where broken statues lie inside the poem
and lone and level sands stretch far away.

Art is a fire, for it burns the heart;
it is a phoenix from the ashes rising.
So do not say it purifies in part;
we are consumed without our realizing
art is a fire, for it burns the heart.

Upon Avon

These muddy waters measuring the light
of that same moon, still round and rolling cold
as once it rolled in autumns dark and bright
when you upon this bank grew up and old—

these waters whisper to the swans that go
and glide across the current to my side;
they whisper you are living even though
the steeple yonder says that you have died.

I know it so. This river overflows
as surely as your Cleopatra's Nile
buoys up her fecund death, as surely grows
Hermione to life all this long while.

When her still statue stirred and stepped in grace,
you after time came swimming to this place.

The Fair Ophelia Hesitates on the Trinity River

after Michele Simonsen and Tim Webb

She looks as if she is about to go onstage,
recalling her lines ("How does your honor?")
before she floats into the dark
waves of performance.

But soft, her cue has not yet come,
and the wind and current keep
eternal house without her.

The rock shelving on the bank
provides the perfect seats within this theater,
where nothing yet is happening
except for the soliloquy of a barren snag.

"To be or not to be?" it says.
But clearly it has chosen to be,
a white angle of resistance,
while our heroine waits, and waits, and waits,
testing the waters like a willow.

Elizabeth Barrett Contemplates the Sonnets from the Portuguese

I stopped at 44, counting the ways that far,
having reached, I suppose, the ends
of being and ideal grace, and
how much more could he want?

God knows I had flattered him
far too much already,
and the silver iterance has to end
somewhere. Master-hands my eye—

if I hadn't dragged him to Italy,
he never would have learned to write.
And do you think his last duchess
simply appeared out of nowhere?

Some days I was afraid to smile
at the one-armed Florentine
who dropped by to demand the rent.
As if *his* royalties paid the bills!

And his carrying on at those séances—
bumping the table with his knees
and then laughing uproariously.
This was my rescuing angel?

Still, Shakespeare had his 154,
and I not even a third of that.
But did Shakespeare ever admit the impediment
of a single object for his affections?

First there was that master-mistress pretty boy,
then his luscious dark lady of lust in action—
I even wonder if something wasn't
going on secretly with that rival poet.

So, 44, a good number—a round one,
and, yes, an even one—but as odd
as the curls on his Victorian brow,
as odd as love's eternity.

A Wish

The way that Tennyson once read his poems,
deep-chested music surging in surprise
from that dark mind, that troubled mind at peace,
the hollow *ohs* and *ahs* that spun release—

I would have liked to hear him, sit beside
the sofa when he bent to toll the words,
for then I should have known him by his voice,
the hovering between his chance and choice.

I would have listened quietly, and once
or twice have nodded sagely as we do
when peal and sense unite inside our grasp,
an oiled gate swung soft upon the hasp.

The page is silent, pouring day to day
its speech upon the vastness of the night.
We cannot sound him, though we see him spelt,
But echo moves and answers, *I have felt.*

Dinah Morris Digresses in
Her Evening Sermon on the Green

Dear people, the gospels tell us
that when the Lord entered her village,
Martha received him into her home.

She *received* him, friends, that busiest body
in the scriptures, the first of us all
who hope to receive him into our hearts.

Martha was the first to choose that good portion,
and just because she did not have the stomach
for a second helping, who are we

to judge her for that? To eat the bread
and then to drink the wine as well—
is that not more than anyone can do in the flesh?

David Douglas Writes Home Concerning the California Mission Fathers, 1832

I am no friend to Catholic belief—
and yet I wish to speak empirically.
The fathers gave me hospitality,
excess of it and courtesies beside—
the kind that can be felt but not expressed.
There were no bickerings, no ill attempts
to change my faith (the usual complaint
of travelers among their synagogues).
When with them I was under no restraint—
my time was as my own, feast day or fast.
These men of God, these good men gave to me
a warm bed always and, to eat and drink,
the best of that broad land. A more upright
and honorable class I never knew.
(Of course they dwell in error, but their errors
are but the errors of their profession.)
Well-schooled they are; except for one or two,
they all speak Latin fluently, and though
pronunciation be a diverse thing
between one from Auld Reekie and Madrid,
it yet gave little trouble. They do love
the sciences too well to think it strange
to see one go so far in quest of grass.

Colin Campbell Cooper

One-hundred-year-old clouds—
are they the same
as those I see across the ridge today?

They are less temperate,
so full, so like a manuscript
discovered in a box made for croquet.

First Rain

falls the morning before Halloween, cold and thick.
I interrupt my eight-o'clock to drive downtown
for jury duty, park five blocks away, leap and dodge

the swollen gutters to join a swirl of citizen peers.
Three of them I recognize: a local physical therapist
who is also a famous rockclimber, a neighbor who teaches

computer science at city college, and an elder poet
from the university. Sunday, he stood in our kitchen
and read us his poem about the September 11 attacks,

a poem on the model of "This Is the House That Jack Built,"
a poem full of maidens all forlorn. But I am wrong
about the neighbor. She is actually a more distant

acquaintance, an artist whose husband manages
our retirement funds: I would make a better juror
than a witness. During a break, the climber tells me

about his latest, a 5.11 spire to the north of Whitney—
a route so far beyond my skill it fails to stir
my latent envy. Is this the meaning of middle age?

I wish him well, recall that once he broke his back
on talus at the foot of Half Dome. Because of his own
ailing back, the elder poet gets a deferral. The climber

somehow falls away, the artist brushes past me
for another courtroom. Outside, the rain makes
bubbles on the parking lot under a pepper tree,

and the rest of us spread out like rainbowed streaks of oil,
awaiting our chance at some small justice, the solace
of autumn, the hallowing of a dark new year.

FDNY

And did they climb those stairs?
   They did. Oh yes, they did.
      Oh yes, they did.

And did they find their duty there?
   They did. Oh yes, they did.

And when those towers fell, what then?
   What did become of them?
      What then?

They kept on climbing. Yes, they did.
   With all their heart, with all their will,
      They kept on climbing still.

And are they climbing even now?
   And are they climbing now?

Oh yes, they are. They're climbing there.
   On stairs and towers everywhere,
      In boots and hats and heavy fare
         They keep on climbing through that air
      To do their duty there.

And do they still, with right good will?
   Oh yes, they do, for me, for you.
      They keep on climbing for they care
      To do their dusty duty there.

And shall we bless them full and fair?
   We shall, oh yes, we shall, we shall,
      We shall bless them everywhere.

We do bless them full and fair,
   Because oh yes, because oh yes,
      Because they still do climb those stairs.

On the 225th Year of Mission Santa Barbara

After our house burned down in the Tea Fire,
we rented a place on Laguna Street a few blocks
below the Mission. In the mornings I'd walk
the dog to the rose garden and through the high grass
of the meadow underneath the bell towers,
desperately in need of their blessing.

I took comfort in knowing they had been there
for a long time, shadowing others in their search
for certainty, for something in their lives that would stay.
Oh, I know those towers crumbled in an earthquake in 1925,
and whatever had preceded them was reduced
to rubble in 1812. And I also know that the Chumash
were not altogether grateful to be herded into these precincts
and forced to build that fern-covered dam on the creek.

And the long abuse of those boys at the school—
I know about that too. But driving home from work
that winter, I often chose the longer route
that brought me down the canyon to that graceful turn
around those towers rising above the rusty leaves
of sycamore in the last of the sun, my gaze
falling across the lawn to the tile rooftops of our city,
the ocean beyond, the islands glinting like a promise.

And I would think of those many friars, most of them
so patient and humble, so full of faith, so dedicated
to those who came to place their burdens on the warm stone
of these steps that lead out from that sanctuary
to the rest of this beautiful, suffering world.

Notes

The epigraph is quoted from the New Revised Standard Version.

"Gift" was written in response to the poem "Peaches & Cream," by Barry Spacks, from his book *Regarding Women* (Cherry Grove Collections, 2004).

"Seconds" was written for the wedding of my father and stepmother, David and Ruth Willis, in May 2006, after the deaths of their first spouses.

"Burn Victims," with other poems in this volume, recalls the aftermath of the Santa Barbara Tea Fire of November 2008.

"Almost Spring at the Hut" revisits Ostrander Ski Hut in the Yosemite backcountry, built by the Civilian Conservation Corps in 1941.

"Bubbs Creek" is for Sharon.

"Los Prietos" was written on the site of the Los Prietos Civilian Public Service Camp on the Santa Ynez River near Santa Barbara. Among the conscientious objectors stationed there from 1942–1944 was the poet William Stafford.

"ROTC, 1974" recalls a time at Wheaton College when all freshman men were required to take part in morning drill in uniform.

"Juneau Icefield, 1973" recalls student days on the Juneau Icefield Research Program directed by Maynard M. Miller.

"Little Ruaha River, 1998" recalls a visit to a Houghton College program directed by Jon Arensen in the central highlands of Tanzania.

"Croquet at Hengrave, 1992" recalls a semester with students from Westmont College at Hengrave Hall, a Tudor manor house near Bury St.

Notes

Edmunds. At the time, it was staffed as a retreat center by the Sisters of the Assumption.

"Assessment": For a copy of the report that should be stapled to this poem, please contact the Western Association of Schools and Colleges, 533 Airport Boulevard, Suite 200, Burlingame, CA 94010.

"Dido" was written in response to a painting of the same title by Charles Garabedian (2006).

"Art Is a Fire" was written for the installation of Judy L. Larson as the R. Anthony Askew Chair in Art, Westmont College, in January 2009.

"The Fair Ophelia Hesitates on the Trinity River" was written in response to the photograph "Above Water #7," by Michele Simonsen and Tim Webb (2012).

"A Wish" concludes with an affirmation from Tennyson's *In Memoriam* 124 (1850).

"Dinah Morris Digresses in Her Evening Sermon on the Green" borrows as its mouthpiece the young Methodist preacher from George Eliot's novel *Adam Bede* (1859).

"David Douglas Writes Home Concerning the California Mission Fathers, 1832" is a conflation of several letters written by the botanist to friends and family. *Auld Reekie* is a Scottish nickname for Edinburgh that refers to the coal smoke that wreathed the town.

Colin Campbell Cooper (1856–1937) was an American painter noted for his landscapes and cloudscapes. He retired and died in Santa Barbara.

"FDNY" was written for a ceremony of remembrance at the Santa Barbara County Courthouse on the tenth anniversary of the September 11 attacks.

"On the 225th Year of Mission Santa Barbara" was written at the request of Sister Susan Blomstad. The Mission was founded by Father Junipero Serra in 1786.

www.ingramcontent.com/pod-product-compliance
Lightning Source LLC
Chambersburg PA
CBHW022115090426
42743CB00008B/859